HOW I GOT OVER
An Overcomer's Anthology

Iris P. Bryant
Sharon Garnett   Tameka M. King
Wendy W. Melvin   Eulanda Thorne

Mattie's Seed Publishing
Greensboro, NC

©2018 Iris P. Bryant. All Rights Reserved.
ISBN: 978-0991647941
Published by Mattie's Seed Publishing

All rights reserved. No part of this book may be reproduced or transmitted in any form or by any means, mechanical or electronic, including photocopying or recording or by any information storage and retrieval system, or transmitted by email without permission except in the case of brief quotations embodied in critical reviews or articles.

Scripture references are from the King James Version of the Holy Bible unless otherwise noted.

Cover design by: K&T Graphics
Edited by: Critique Editing Services, LLC

Dedication

To Kimberly Louise Bowden, a true sister and friend. May her life,
legacy, and love of words always inspire others to dream big.

"We are hard pressed on every side, but not crushed; perplexed, but not in despair; persecuted, but not abandoned, struck down, but not destroyed."
2 Corinthians 4:8-9

Table of Contents

Acknowledgements 9
Introduction 11
In His Strength 13
He Saw the Best in Me 21
The Freedom of Forgiveness 30
I Choose to Love 44
From Rejected to Redeemed 58

Acknowledgements

Thank You, Lord for the gracing us with the anointing of the overcomer. We are honored that You chose to bless us to share our messages of hope. May this work bring honor to You.

Special thanks to Gwendolyn Best, Shecna Murphy, Alyssa Womble, Adrienne Carter, Deon Melvin, Bryan Peterson, and LaDedra Shackleford for your assistance with this project. May God continue to bless the works of your hands as you operate in the spirit of excellence.

Thanks to Karen Rodgers and Natasha Miller for your editorial and design services. We were blessed to have the opportunity to work with you.

To Debra Cheek and Timiel Dewberry your love, support, and prayers have been invaluable.

To our families, thanks for the love and continued support.

Introduction

"And they overcame them by the blood of the Lamb, and by the word of their testimony; and they loved not their lives unto death."
Revelations 12:11

The testimonies contained in this book are meant to show the awesome power of God. These women have endured great challenges and setbacks, moments where they questioned their faith, and longed for God's deliverance. Through it all, God has been faithful and just.

The women featured in this book entered a room as complete strangers with one goal: to share their testimonies so that others can be free. They were gathered for an opportunity to take photos for this book's cover, but I watched them grow and become sisters in the brief time we were together. Strangers have become sisters who have boldly stood in the gap for each other. They have interceded for and encouraged each other. They have been each other's cheerleaders and sounding boards. They have grown in grace and in love because they shared their most personal experiences and their hearts with each other.

I have the same prayer for you that I had the day we gathered for the first time. May the life stories of triumph from these women bring healing, restoration, and deliverance to you. If you never meet them or never have the opportunity to be in their presence, when you finish this book, you will have connected with sisters with powerful testimonies of how God brought them over. I am honored to call each of these women my sister warriors. I am thankful that God allowed our paths to cross, but most of all I am humbled they entrusted me with their pearls.

IN HIS STRENGTH
Sharon Garnett

I want to thank God for allowing me to have a tongue that is the pen of a ready writer that He may speak His words through me. All glory and honor belong to Him for giving me the strength to tell my story.

One of my earliest and most enjoyable memories was when my grandpa, Hein Garnett, a landscaper, would take me to work with him. When I turned five, my Saturday mornings were spent picking up sticks in the yards that he was taking care of. To me it was more than just picking up sticks because I began to see God's creation in those little sticks. While he was working, my imagination took me to places beyond those yards in Augusta, Georgia. Looking back, that's when I began to develop an anointing to see purpose in things that other people consider useless.

What I did understand was that spending those Saturdays with Grandpa got me out of the house. I really thank God for my grandpa!

There were eight of us and my home life was not easy. We went through a lot watching our mother trying to find love. She wanted to be appreciated, but she always ran into hurt.

After leaving the jobs with my grandpa, I was able to escape at home by finding sticks in the back yard and building more of my special creations. There were little things that upset me, like every time I made one of those same stick creations at home, my sister would come and tear it down. Even though she tore them all down, I continued to build! This prepared me for the attacks that often come from the enemy. He comes to kill, steal, and destroy, but I have to remain at a place of peace and remember all the joy that I have from using my hands for the glory of God.

I later found out that it was the enemy who was attacking the works of my hands and not my sister.

My mama worked hard to provide for us, but it was very hard to get us everything we needed. During Christmas, Grandpa would always help out and make sure that we had Christmas presents. One Christmas my Grandpa bought me a little red fire truck. I was happy, but my sisters and cousin tore up my fire truck before I could really enjoy it!

Their actions caused me to become angry and I immediately wanted to fight. Sadly, home wasn't the only place that I had to fight opposition.

Although I loved working in the yard with Grandpa and playing with new creations, there was one place that I hated—school! My problems did not start at school, they began at the bus stop. Every day I would be picked on because of my size, my hair and my clothes. I got so tired of being called "fat" and "nappy head" that I told my mom I wanted to go to school, but I just didn't want to have to go to the bus stop. What happened at the bus stop made it hard for me to want to learn once I arrived at school. From first grade to fifth grade, my mama struggled to get me out of the house in the morning.

When I saw that my mama was not going to give in to my wishes to skip the bus stop, I would miss the bus on purpose and stay home so I would not get picked on.

I grew up when the kids in the neighborhood were everybody's kids, so when the ladies saw me waiting around the corner until the bus passed, they would tell my mama that I did not go to school that day. I would always go back home and eat and go back to sleep. Even when I got in trouble, I always said that was better than going to school to get picked on.

Today, those children are called bullies, but back then we just called them mean! I felt that I would always be called names and that there was no one to protect me. Only God knows how badly I longed for protection.

I will never forget my seventh grade year. There was a janitor who was always in the hallway looking at us young girls. He knew that most of us had not eaten breakfast before we left home, so he used to give us candy and soda pop. We did not realize that it was a setup.

This pattern continues to present itself today—believing that you have to give something to get something. That stays on my mind all the time because I was thinking he was a good person, but when he gave me the soda pop and candy, he would end up touching my breast.

As my body began to develop, my mom and the neighborhood ladies thought I was out messing with some little boy. I wanted to tell her to go to the school house and tell the principal the janitor was bribing the young girls with cookies, candies, and sodas in return for touching their bodies.

I believe I was not the only one. The hate that I had for school intensified. What was the use of going to school? I did not want to deal with that so early in the morning.

One of my cousins and I used to talk about not going to school and when we got old enough we were going to quit. We knew that at the age of 16 we were leaving school.

We still had a ways to go before we got to that age, so we started skipping school on a regular basis. We would wait for Mama to go to work, but soon the pattern that began in school started following me home. Cousins were given the responsibility of watching me as well. They fondled my body, eventually taking advantage of me by having sex with me. I never knew when I lost my virginity back then because I thought that it was alright. Everywhere I went that evil followed me because I did not have anyone to watch over me or protect me.

I did not realize God's love and grace kept me from any kind of disease that could have taken over my body at a young age. Many times I just wanted to die. I often wondered what I was living for?

There was so much that was going on in my body, from constant nosebleeds to other signs of stress. I was dealing with adult problems that nobody knew about. No one knew because I was afraid to tell it.

As a result of the constant nosebleeds, my mom and older ladies in the neighborhood would take brown paper bags soaked in vinegar and place them underneath my nose to stop the bleeding. I despise vinegar to this day because of that experience. I remember the torture from the children at the bus stop, the fondling from my cousin, and the terrible vinegar and how I didn't feel like I was fit for anything.

I understand more today how when we hold stuff in, it affects us in the long run because we are afraid to tell it. It is my desire to encourage people not to be afraid to tell. I am anointed to tell it now. A lot of people don't like to hear it, but that's part of my purpose. I am anointed to tell, I will no longer hold in anything else. At my age, now that I have learned, I will not let anything bother me.

Because I felt ashamed of my body and what I was going through, I could not wait until I turned 16 so that I could drop out of school. Little did I know my life would only get worse. I didn't learn anything in school and I longed for the attention of my teachers. I didn't ask for extra help and I didn't get it. Each report card that I brought home resulted in a beating from Mama. I never made grades above a C and Mama was not happy.

I decided that the only way for me to get help at school and stay out of trouble with Mama was to ask to be in the exceptional needs classes. As a student in the exceptional needs classroom, I was able to receive the attention that I longed for. My teacher spent time with me, working patiently with me until she knew I understood the material, but I didn't know that unwelcome attention was lurking in the background.

My grades improved, and my mama was happy about the grades, but no one knew that my enrollment in these classes provided another opening for the giant of molestation to enter my life.

There was a rule in place for exceptional needs students that we had to either ride the bus or wait for someone to pick us up from school. I didn't ride the bus because of the bullies, and my mama was working, so she could not pick me up from school. The same janitor that had touched me inappropriately earlier went to the teacher to tell her that he could take me home. He was seen as doing a good deed, but those rides home led to acts of molestation. I would not tell my mama what was happening because I was afraid I would get into more trouble. I kept this to myself until the day that I decided to tell my cousin. When she asked me what I was going to do, I told her I decided that I could not go back to school. Although my plan was to drop out of school at 16, I made a decision to leave earlier because I thought that was the only way for me to escape the bullying and molestation.

In spite of what I endured at school, God protected me with his strength.

As I was able to spend more time in my mom's house, I saw alcohol abuse from my uncles, aunties, and my brothers. Their use of alcohol opened other doors where sexual sin came into our lives. Their dependency on alcohol caused them to cast off restraints in other areas of their lives. They did not use discretion with their sexual partners, and things that should have taken place privately—or not at all—were done openly in the presence of the younger ones.

This just shows how generational curses open doors that must be closed in prayer. I witnessed so many things at a young age without understanding what was going on. I did not know what was right from what was wrong.

Finally, I had enough! I am grateful for my Heavenly Father saving me and keeping me from a miserable life of sin and abuse. His hand of protection was on me even though I did not realize it. He has given me the spirit of discernment, so I can recognize what the spirit of molestation as well as the spirit of incest can do to a person's life.

I decided I had to get away from Augusta. I knew if I didn't I would die, so I made up my mind to leave. I didn't know where I was going, but when I climbed out of that window, I knew I was going to go somewhere. Then I heard about Job Corps and I decided to join. That was the best thing I could have ever done.

Back then I felt like there was no hope. My body was so abused and was damaged on the inside. I never felt that I could be loved and when I did find it, it was taken away. The spirit of molestation and coming from an incestuous past brought about a damaged marriage and a mind of fear. It was security that I wanted, and to be loved without being abused. But going through life being strong, God blessed me with two wonderful kids. God has strengthened me to tell my story as He is my strength, making me whole and complete in Him where I live and move and have my being. I have my mind back, I have my body back. I can live a happy, complete life and I don't have to run anymore to try to save my life. I'm free and when I gave it to my Lord and Savior, He taught me how to live again.

I have made sure that my house is a place of peace and refuge for others. In order for God to forgive me, I had to forgive those who wronged me. I have had the opportunity to minister to family members and usher healing into their lives. The curse is broken, and I will continue to walk in wholeness and complete deliverance.

I thank God because if it was not for His strength that brought me through, I don't know where I would be. But thanks be to Him for allowing me to know now that He was with me every step of the way. It was all in His plan and all in His purpose. To God be the glory.

Sharon Garnett is passionate about sharing the Gospel of Jesus Christ with everyone she encounters. She is a crafter who sells handmade jewelry, home décor, soaps and lotions. A native of Augusta Georgia, she currently resides in eastern North Carolina.

HE SAW THE BEST IN ME
Wendy Warren Melvin

It was a great year for me in that I had received a promotion on my job. I had been in Transportation less than a year and I was given a new position. There I was not long out of high school with a little over two years of community college and I was being promoted to Section Leader of Transportation. This meant having ladies under me and it also meant having a new pay level. Things were really moving fast once I assumed the position. At times the responsibility mixed with my level of maturity made me giggle inside. I knew that there was no way I was supposed to be there. There was no way a 23-year-old young woman with no prior corporate experience should be assuming this task. This had to be the hand of the Higher pushing me along this path and I was loving it.

The pride within began to seep outward. I was oblivious to the response that would follow. In my mind the world was beginning to look and feel differently than the world I grew up in. The words my earthly father told me began to play back in my head but somehow, they didn't apply to me, or so I thought. "In this world, there are very few people who have your back and your parents are two of them." Anyone who knew my father knew that he told you how it was whether you liked it or not. I had no idea that in order to climb the corporate ladder you had to step on others along the way. I worked for the largest pork-producing company in the world. The work was scrutinized and perfected. Sometimes the pressure was so intense it felt like my head would explode. The ladies under me, some younger and some older, had more experience than me yet somehow, I was in charge. The longer we worked together the more intense our work relationships became. We began to nitpick at each other to the point that we would find ourselves looking for employment elsewhere. Here I was doing the same thing to these ladies that I loathed the days prior to my promotion. How did I get here? Who was I becoming? I refused to look at this person even though it was me. I knew my father was right because I was one of those people who didn't have anyone's back but my own.

Day after day, week after week, the relationships would grow more volatile. My friend whom I trusted to do the daily work was growing impatient with me. I was so preoccupied with the perfection of the work that the people behind the work faded into the background. The thought of being able to perform above the rest of the group took over my day and night dreams. I learned all of the reports: daily, weekly and monthly. Determination became my driving force. Knowing that the more tasks I could perform, the more valuable I would be. Self-absorption was becoming the fabric of choice. Stepping away from others into my own world was the new path I chose to take. Even though I would be sitting across from one of the ladies in a cubical, I wouldn't even know she was there until we took breaks or went to lunch. I remember praying to God for strength before the promotion and after it came I felt strong, but for the first time I felt alone.

After losing my friend to another job at a different company, I began to realize that my style of leading was not working. The giggle inside was turning to tears and sadness. I had to do something to redeem myself. I had become self-absorbed and conceited. To keep my mind off of the trouble I was facing, I decided to take a second job for a retail store. There was a motive behind the madness.

Staying busy was a much-needed task. I had to keep my mind off of my position and the ladies that had left my group. I applied to a retail store for a cashier position with the intention of earning extra money and getting more experience. Deep down inside I wanted to seek employment elsewhere. I did get the job and it was only a couple of months before I received a promotion to count cash in the cash office. This was a big deal because I would have gained experience counting cash, with codes and combinations. This could open doors for me in a big way down the road of life. Working two jobs was getting stressful. Leaving one job at 4:00 p.m. and clocking in at the other at 5:00 p.m. until the store closed was the routine. I worked this schedule for months and I was careful not to complain about the stress or being tired. Complaining could have caused termination, especially at the office. My mind was always on work and what was happening at work.

It was one of those mornings when I couldn't decide what to wear to work. The temperature outside was a balmy 68 degrees at 6:15 a.m. The dress code at the office was strict. Shorts were not an option, so a skirt and blouse were my outfit of choice. The time was closer to 6:35 a.m. and I was running late. I was traveling down Boykin Bridge Road going at the very least 55 mph. I remember grabbing my seatbelt as I approached the bottom of Boykin Lakes. I approached the intersection and remember saying, "Oh my God, he is not going to stop." I also remember thinking that I was going to die and asking God to forgive me for my sins. The next thing I knew a stranger was helping me out of my seatbelt because my car was smoking. He told me that the ambulance was on the way.

That accident caused a chain of events that reshaped my life. I had maxofacial injuries to my lower jaw that resulted in a nine-hour surgery. My back injuries were not apparent until a year later. I underwent four surgeries on both hands. My body experienced a major change, going from 120 pounds down to 80 pounds due to being unable to eat because of the jaw surgeries. The mental changes were unbearable, and I felt like I had no control over my life.

I began having long talks with God. I remember having a dream during this time, and in the dream, I saw many of my friends and some family members through a window. I could see them, but they couldn't see me. I could hear them, but they couldn't hear me. I heard them clearly and woke up out of the dream. The things that they were saying in my dream about me were so hurtful. I asked God, "What could I possibly learn from this dream?" The answer was revealed to me quickly. The next day I ran into one of the people in my dream and he said, "I thought you were faking because it was an accident that was not your fault." My response was, "Really? I guess the doctors and surgeons must be operating on me just for fun." The people in my life who I thought had my back really didn't. I was in this battle alone, just me and God.

After the jaw surgery I was ready to get better so that I could get back to work. The doctor said I would only be out of work for 8 weeks. I was so hopeful and ready to be me again. A couple of weeks passed, and I was still recovering. I was really weak from not being able to eat anything solid. Living on Ensure was not like eating a meal, it was just liquid nutrition. This was also affecting me mentally. I could see food, smell food, touch food, but I couldn't eat food. This was so hard because my family still ate like normal, and around me at that.

Four months would pass before I would even be able to swallow blended foods, but this was a much needed step up from drinking Ensure. The maxofacial surgeries were rough, but the other surgeries that followed were no cakewalk either. I managed to get through each procedure with no complications. The pain in my lower back and right leg was getting worse. I ended up having three surgeries on my lower back over a period of two years. Pain medicine, muscle relaxers, anti-inflammatories, and physical therapy were all a part of my daily routine. My surgeons also referred me to a pain clinic in order to keep my pain levels at a minimum. Again I was thinking that soon I would be as good as new, and I could get back to work. There was a problem with my thinking. I was now a little over 80 pounds, couldn't wear heels anymore and sitting, walking and standing for long periods of time was painful. I had to get this figured out; I had to get back to work. Financially I needed to work. I held my first real job at age 14 and have worked ever since. My medical leave at work was changed from one year to indefinite. Once my FMLA (Family and Medical Leave Act) ran out, I was terminated by my employer. This was crushing to me because I had hopes of getting back to normal.

"Well since your back is so messed up, having children is not an option for you." The doctor at Duke Medical Center looked at my MRIs from the surgeries and told me that a life of steroid injections was what I needed to get used to. I also remember him making a joke that those injections in my tailbone would be just as painful as giving birth. I was so depressed; it seemed like before I could heal from one thing something else would happen. I remember standing in the prayer line at church, asking God to have mercy on me and heal my back so that I could get back to work. There I stood in the prayer line with my right arm behind the small of my back clenching my fist, asking for prayer. "Remove your hand from behind your back and give me your hands." This was the instruction given to me by my pastor. Time stood still in that moment. The prayer from the preacher was one of healing and trust. I was told to trust and believe God for healing. I was told to believe that I was healed at that very moment. My pastor said that as long as I believed, I would receive. That Sunday I felt better. I knew God had heard my prayer and an answer was given.

The surgeries and pain took a toll on me mentally. Could I walk in the healing that the preacher said I would experience? Would I be able to have children? How could I help myself get better? I asked God to help me with a feeling I had, the feeling that I didn't deserve to be healed. I can honestly say that at times I felt like I was reaping the harvest of seeds I had sown.

The pain clinic had become a home away from home. The therapist would ask me about my pain but also about what made it worse or what made it better. I would laugh and say, "Only in my dreams is the pain better because in my dreams, I can't feel the pain." I could talk to my doctors about my pain but trying to talk to family and friends about it was impossible. No one understood me, and no one could relate. It was really hard to understand why people didn't understand; however, pain is invisible.

As time passed I longed to have a normal life and that included having a child. I did remember what my doctors said, but I knew that all things are possible through Christ Jesus. I decided I would at least ask my doctor again and see if by chance he felt I was stronger and could carry a baby without complication. The answer was different in that he said, "Yes, physically you could carry a baby, but there would likely be major complications." I decided against it and that's when I decided I had to do something to help with the longing to become a mother.

God knew my heart's desire because a few weeks later a friend of my husband said he was looking for a babysitter. I jumped at the chance to help them out. I was so happy that God would allow me to see how being a mother felt. The highlight of my days became keeping this baby boy. This child was only nine weeks old, so I really got a feel for motherhood, and I fell in love. My pain was not in vain. Somehow I knew this was my calling. I thought maybe I was right where God needed me to be to help out a friend and to help fill the void in my heart. We developed a bond and I was finally feeling like my life had true purpose once again. The love grew as did this precious baby boy. Zack was approaching age four and his dad was talking preschool. I knew that he would qualify because he was such a smart toddler. I couldn't bear knowing that he was going to be leaving me soon.

I remember getting sick thinking about it. My body was changing, and I thought, *Ok, maybe this is a mind thing.* At 6:00 p.m. every evening I would find myself in the bathroom hugging the toilet. What in the world was going on? I made an appointment to see my doctor and he told me to go see my OBGYN because it could be a female issue since I was not only nauseated but also feeling abdominal cramps. The date was May 4th and my doctor said, "You are pregnant, and I need you to stop all pain medication immediately." Two days later I called my doctor and told him that I tried to stop all pain medication, but I couldn't. I was violently sick and shaking and I hurt all over. The nurse told me to come in to the office, so I did. My doctor handed me a referral to Duke OBGYN clinic because he said he would not be able to handle all of the complications that my baby and I would face. I cried as I left his office and I pleaded with God to help us.

Going to Duke Clinic was a degrading experience. I was placed in the same category with other mothers who had addictions. My body was dependent upon the pain medication and I really had no idea that this was even possible. I took all medications as prescribed and had never abused medication. I was drug tested each time I entered the clinic and I felt like somehow, I was failing my unborn child. By then I was approaching my second trimester when I was told that I could lose my baby because of the withdrawals.

The first day without the OxyContin was the worst day of

my life. I stayed in the bathroom nearly all day and finally decided that I couldn't do it. I had to take the pill in order to feel normal again. The nurse on duty at Duke Clinic said that the pill they prescribed was a lower dose, so it would not have the same effect and that they were detoxing me on a scale that was gradual. I felt better about taking the medicine and the guilt went away. At least I was trying. I remember swallowing the pill that afternoon and not even five minutes later it came back up. I couldn't keep it down. It literally came up whole. The next day the same thing happened, but this time when I tried to take it, the taste that it left in my mouth made me so sick. Three days had passed and still I couldn't keep the pills down. My back pain was at a high level again and I felt like I was viewing my life on a movie screen. How could I possibly be pregnant and addicted to medication? I called the nurse and went back to Duke Clinic. My doctor said that the hard part of detox was almost over for me. I didn't understand at all what that meant. She said, "You have gone cold turkey for three days and that was quite an accomplishment." It really never occurred to me what was happening. I was detoxing with God's help alone. She said that there was no real explanation for why I couldn't take the pain medicine since I had taken it for so many years before. I knew that God's plan for this baby was not my plan or the doctor's plan.

    I kept Zack off and on until he qualified for preschool. My heart was once again in agony because he was leaving me. The pain was almost unbearable. It was the best thing for the child but the worst thing for me. I knew I shouldn't feel that way. I was being so selfish. By then I was approaching my eighth month of pregnancy. Our son was due in February, so plans for a baby shower were in the works. The doctors at Duke Clinic were sure that our baby was healthy and that I had gotten off of the pain medication in time. I knew in my heart that they were right, and I was looking forward to his arrival.

We were celebrating Zack's birthday on the 18th of January and I was feeling so much pain in my lower back. I decided to go to the emergency room that night and when I got there I was told I was in labor. They said I should go home and rest because it would be at least 24 to 48 hours before delivery. That night I was so miserable that I could not lay down. I stayed up all night long. The next day we headed back to the hospital. When I arrived the nurse checked me and said it was time to have the baby. Bryson was born on the 19th of January. He was a few weeks early; however, he was healthy. The doctors said I was due on February 7th, but I went into labor on Zack's birthday. That day will always be special to me, and I will never forget Zack's birthday. Only God could have caused that.

My experience in this life so far is that God's plan is not always our plan. This is a small portion of my testimony, there is so much more. My relationship with God is the most precious gift that I have in this life. Through it all I have learned to trust God. He's got me.

Wendy Warren Melvin is a graduate of Lakewood High School in Roseboro, North Carolina. She earned an Associate in Arts degree from Sampson Community College, a Bachelor of Arts from East Carolina University. She is a member of Phi Theta Kappa Honor Society, National Tutoring Association, (NTA), and previously employed as a Tutor for Sampson Community College. She has a love for the elderly in the surrounding communities and a passion for travel. She and her husband have one child.

THE FREEDOM OF FORGIVENESS
Tameka Marable King

I was in the eighth grade when my family changed direction. As I look back on those days, we were a loving family based on the love my parents knew how to offer. We understood the things they did not possess, they could not provide. They were both raised without their fathers and now mine was leaving us. The marriage had come to an end for my parents. I do not know exactly what my older and younger sisters felt; however, I was completely crushed.

My broken heart would lead me to some broken places. Thirteen and going through hormonal changes and now this! I was angry and disappointed too. I felt like it was my fault because I had done nothing to stop their decision. I spent so much time crying secretly. It is like something in you tells you that it is not ok to not be ok. That thinking is dysfunctional. Dysfunctional thinking leads to dysfunctional behavior. I began to have a terrible attitude towards others.

That negative attitude would get me in trouble, in arguments, in fights and in bad relationships. My mom was a hard worker and would often be tired. My dad was my hero. It did not matter how much he failed, I found him to be great. I blamed my mom for the divorce. That was harsh, and I am saddened to think I felt that way. Today I realize that as children you do not always see or hear what is going on. She protected us from their truth.

She provided for us and did her best as a single parent. At

the end of ninth grade, I discovered I was pregnant. Three months after giving birth to my first daughter, my relationship with her father ended. I too was a single parent. I was sixteen years old and by the time my daughter was nine months old, I was pregnant again. My mom was overwhelmed and embarrassed by my actions. She still was there. She still took care of us. She still loved me. I am forever grateful. I was a single mother of two girls, in high school, working part-time, and attending our local community college, my schedule was hectic. My responsibilities seemed mountain high. I was resentful.

I was attending the college at night to ensure I would have enough credits to graduate with my class. Self-destruction was my avenue. I was surrounded by people but feeling alone. My paternal grandmother passed away when my oldest was eight months old and I felt like I died with her. I found myself blaming other relatives for her demise. I thought more could have been done to make sure she was good. I knew she was getting frustrated with life because a couple of weeks before she passed away she told me she was. I used to go by and take her to run errands and sneak liquor in the house. She died due to alcohol poisoning. I felt responsible for that too. The weights were getting heavier each year. I continued to carry them.

The assistance I received from my family helped me to graduate high school on time. I was filled with anger and sadness. I was eighteen years old with two daughters, ages one and two. I was struggling to get by and I knew I needed to hit the workforce soon because my limited thinking was speaking clearly that any more schooling would take too long. I was walking around unaware of the poison that was filling my body from those debilitating emotions. I started working, moved out on my own, and enrolled in the community college against my better judgment.
I spent more time in the game room than in class. By then we

were living in low income housing, receiving benefits for childcare, food, and medical treatment. I decided to get two jobs to be able to furnish my apartment the way I wanted, so I quit school. I know you are thinking, *That is crazy,* and I totally agree. The nineteen-year-old girl who made the decision to do so would fight you because she believed the choice was better.

One of the hardest lessons to learn is that to be able to forgive others we first must learn to forgive ourselves. I say *learn* because forgiveness is not just included in your DNA. When things happen between us and people who we feel have wronged us in any way we must choose to let it go. We do not always know the reason for the actions of those in our lives or even those who may choose not to be. It remains that if we are angry with them, we probably have been angry with ourselves. The decision to release those toxic emotions is liberating.

Most things start in the mind. The actions of other people do not; however. The way we choose to respond will be a thought first. Forgiving yourself takes effort. See, we like to believe that it is easier to accept zero responsibility for the things we take part in, say, or even refuse to do, but it comes down to you and what you feel should be your course of action. I can guarantee you, the longer you hold on to the anger, unforgiveness, and disappointment towards yourself, the longer you are trapped. This trap is internal. People do not see the struggle you are having within yourself daily.

The enemy will make you believe as many lies as he possibly can. He is the Father of Lies. First, release the lies he has put in you to break you down or keep you bound. None of this can be done without Jesus. In our own might we do not have the strength. But He who created us has all power! By His authority, the Spirit that raised Jesus from the dead is living in you. Read Romans 8:11.

Let's examine the first thing I experienced that needed

forgiveness, based on my recollection. As a little girl I was molested. As a young child you do not understand any of the experience. What you do realize is that it is wrong, dirty, a secret, and you likely caused it to occur. These are the first lies the devil will tell you as you simply follow the instructions of the perpetrator. The root of this person's evil may have been at the hands of someone else who did the same thing to them. I kept it a secret until my adult life. During my childhood one close relative was aware but we both kept quiet. This relative was young too. The issue with being exposed to sexual tendencies at the age of four is that it reshapes the direction of your little life. The spirit of perversion enters your sweet soul.

I was such an outgoing child. I was talkative and funny. My molester was a female. I trusted her, but I also feared her. The next realization was that this broken trust would affect all the relationships in my life until healing could begin. I would crave sexual attention and I also believe it brought a sense of shame with each encounter. My relationships were long but dysfunctional. Sex was the chemistry that I looked for. I did not want to be in a serious relationship because I did not trust anyone other than myself. It was also my way of being in control in my mind. Being in control was important because you have zero control over being molested. The manifestation of emotions that follow unresolved hurt, shame, pain, trauma, and betrayal are released into the world through the hurting victim. Hurt people hurt people, especially themselves. I did not revisit that dark place because I had totally blocked it out. Subconsciously the thoughts were there. It just meant I was not fully aware of those thoughts.

I could not get it together. I could not get stable. My choices were poor. My anger was so bad. I was filled with rage. I did not care about other people or their feelings. By the time I was living on my own, things got worse. When I left home I had two beautiful girls to take care of. They saw me up and they saw me down. I had a short fuse. I cursed like a sailor. I took care of them under all circumstances. Two jobs, going without food so they could eat full meals if money was tight, and strict. They were beautiful and smart. They were also total opposites. We grew together. When the girls were eight and nine, I gave birth to my third child. I was twenty-four and unmarried. They all had different fathers, but they all had my last name.

I have no regrets as it relates to parenting. The only issue was I was still a single mom working hard to provide by myself. Those struggles added more emotional baggage to me. Resentment became a neighbor to unforgiveness, which was secretly residing in my mind, heart, and soul. Anger was an anchor to my attitude. People see you, they see what you do, they hear what you do, but they do not know you most of the time. I could not find myself because I needed to revisit the little girl in me who was lashing out through my actions as a young woman. I was always moving, changing jobs, distancing myself from peers and becoming that much more broken.

At the age of twenty-eight, I verbalized the truth. Somehow, I still felt like it was misunderstood or not believed. Bitterness took a back seat to the sister friends who already occupied my internal space. By that time, I was in a relationship with the man who would become my husband. Now let me backtrack just a little. I was going through a period of seeking God at twenty-seven. I first got saved at the age of twenty-one, but was in and out. When I decided to be serious, it was due to constant failure going on in my life. At least I viewed those things as such. I was broken down so bad inside. I hated myself. What God made me aware of was that if I could not love myself, I would not be capable of loving others properly. That goes for children, parents, lover, spouse or friends. How can you give something you do not have? It is impossible. First, you must admit what you are dealing with. God placed a special coworker in my life.

I was always blessed with good jobs and I was very easy to get along with. When I clocked out though, the beast would surface. I had absolutely no patience. But as the Lord used this beautiful vessel to constantly speak life into me she also shared the dark truths about the changes God desired for me to make. You need to be open to hearing and receiving correction from God. It is truly because of His love that we are corrected. She poured so much into me. I am forever grateful. She was selfless. I say that to say that sometimes we may encounter people who are broken, but let us not forget, to get where we are, someone took out the time to minister, be patient and pray for us.

As I desired to grow in God and become who I was supposed to be, I was praying that he would send a man who would love me, love my children as his own, and be strong enough to shut someone down in his confidence of who I am, not who I was before he met me. Having children by different people does not make me less of a mom. It does not make me a slut. People have had more than three partners but may have no children. So that does not make them better than or worse than me. I am not ashamed because today I realize it was a part of my journey. The call on your life will take you through highs and lows. Those stages are meant to build you. Sometimes we are broken down to be built up better than before. Embrace it. If you forget the eggs while baking a cake, it will not turn out right. It will not taste good either. Our experiences belong to us and they are the ingredients we need for our purpose recipe. It is tailored to our fit.

My husband was the man I prayed for. He was everything I did not like or want. So, ladies, please do not reject your Boaz looking for a Bozo. We started out as friends and shared countless conversations daily. I asked God to help me be who I was supposed to be. I prayed that He would allow me to see myself the way that He saw me. God created me, so He knows me in and out. That is why you become vulnerable, broken, and empty. That low place positions you for the best plays of your life, but they are only your best plays if you're led by the Spirit.

I was twenty-seven, and my children were eleven, nine, and two. Phillip had a two-year-old son as well. Quite the long shot for someone who was so hard on herself. For someone who was just finding out that it was vital that she forgive herself and then forgive those who have wronged her. In doing so God would be able to forgive her sins. Now this new revelation was a hard pill to swallow. First, I did not realize the root of the problems all these years. It was revealed through prayer. I asked the Lord to bring to the surface all the things in me that caused me to be who I was that needed to be removed.

Initially I thought, *How could that be the cause of all this chaos in my life?* I also thought, *How did this shift to the back of my mind all these years?* Here comes the shovel as God begins to help you come out of this dark, filthy place. Please understand, each step took time. I did not do any of these things overnight. I did not heal overnight. I did not forgive overnight. My life was changing though. I was happier and that helped my children for sure. I sat my girls down because they were old enough to understand. I apologized for who I had been and who I had not been able to be. Undeniably, I gave them all I could give that was in me at the time. They were loving, innocent, and quick to forgive. I was overprotective of them. I did not leave them with many people. I did not allow them to sit in anyone's lap. No matter what. This was an attempt to keep them safe; although, I refused to associate it with anything I had experienced. I figured I was just a cautious mom.

Early on I did give the talk about body parts, names of body parts, and what inappropriate touching was. I also shared these things with my son when he could understand. It is important that your children are aware. I explained to them they would never be in trouble or blamed if those things occurred. I expressed how necessary it was to tell me even if they were threatened. Do not be afraid to have these conversations with your children because we are their first teachers. They will not know if we do not educate them on the different dangers life can bring. Things that we do not always understand. Yet understanding that it is alright to not always have answers.

My husband was my husband from the beginning. In my email, as I stored his information in the section for nickname, I typed MY HUSBAND in all caps. We had only been talking for a month. I do not know why I typed that because it was my belief that I would never get married. I had no desire to. I did not feel I could trust myself or anyone else on the level marriage would require. Healing said otherwise. Forgiveness opened the door of possibility. I walked through it. God was leading the way. This was the next big area where I would have to exercise forgiveness.

In the early stages of our relationship, Phillip was not always entirely honest. Well, of course for me that equated to a full-blown lie. We dated for five years before we got married. During that time, we talked every single day by text only if I was trying to call it quits. There was a seven-day period of an I-do-not-think-this-is-it type of break he initiated. Well actually, on the seventh day he texted me 88 times, expressing what he felt over that pass week and that it was the worse week of his life. Baby, I was like *Yes, Lord!* I would get so mad at him for the petty mess he did. That was how I knew my life was changing. I was certain God was answering my prayers. I was praying to be patient, forgiving, trusting and loving. Be careful what you pray for. To be strengthened on any level requires repetition and training.

The trials we faced in the beginning included baggage we

brought in. There I was trying to find my new self. In the process, I had fallen in love for the first time while loving myself. God has a way so much sweeter than we could ask for or imagine. The ability to love yourself can only happen if you are willing to stand in your truth. That includes the good and bad. We are changed by the experiences that we have in life. I never imagined that one person could meet every need, satisfy my soul, challenge me, encourage me, and provide for me the way he was willing. God was working on me hard. I know I was a hard nut to crack. I fought kicking and screaming to change my ways on my own.

The reality is I could not do it. I was up one day and down the next. I was suffering from depression. Depression is tough to battle. I began to gain weight, not to mention I smoked a pack of cigarettes a day. I would vent to my patients who were always venting to me. I was going through many challenges even after meeting Phillip. I journaled daily because it was therapeutic for me. I chose to have few friends because I still did not fully trust other people. It is hard to convince someone that you are real or true if they have made up their mind that you might be a liar. That was how I felt. Everyone lied. People were fake. People would easily betray you. I believe those were some of the effects from becoming a teen mom. Let me revisit that time in my life.

You are trusting of people and the things they tell you when you just want that attention. Becoming a parent as a teen is nothing you can be prepared for. You may be physically prepared, but your level of understanding is not quite where it should be. I did not understand that my life was going to be changed forever. I lived day to day. I was irresponsible and careless. I wanted to look cute and have fun. I was selfish. My mom and older sister were so good with helping me out. My mom was beyond the pain I had caused her. All while being unaware of the pains I had been struggling with. Sometimes you may question, *If I could go back and change things, would I?* My answer is no.

My experiences not only grew my character but will be a teacher by testimony to countless others. I want to help people all over the world to find the greatness that lies in them. We get wrapped in layers. Those layers must be peeled back like an onion. Somewhere beneath all the walls you have built up over time is the sweet, seasoned, flavorful you, ready to be resurrected. We know that in order for a resurrection to take place, there will have to be a crucifixion. Peel and kill those layers as they come off. You must be willing to find out the truth about the walls you think are protecting you underneath. See, the onion is covered to protect the inside, the core, so that we can chop it and add it to our food for seasoning. It just makes good food taste even better. Your core contains the real you. The you before the depression, suicide attempts, deceit, lies, anger, molestation, domestic violence, verbal abuse, and anything else the enemy threw your way. The devil can glimpse into our future enough to know he does not want us to get there.

Too bad for him because when God is for us, who can be against us? Correct, not a single being. It's clear that weapons will form, but they shall not prosper. I constantly give thanks for that. If the enemy had his way, you would be eliminated. That is why your experiences seem so tough. You contain so much power. Power that we witness in others but dare not believe that it could be in us. Looking back over your life and the things that you have made it out of, see it clearly. There is so much work to do. The work is well worth the end results.

I had to forgive myself for becoming a mom to my beautiful children but not being in relationships that were healthy to begin with. In retrospect, I understand that more so than not, we are what we see, not what we say. Therefore, if the process to heal begins earlier, we can set standards for ourselves. We can set goals. We can love who we are. You are not born knowing anything. Everything is learned. I choose to teach to the best of my ability. I choose to share, encourage, and help others along the way. I cannot let my trials and temptations go to waste. God chooses those He can trust.

The way God knows He can trust you is based on your ability to obey Him. Obedience is the game changer. I found that it is hard when you lack discipline. Discipline is the practice of being trained or raised to obey rules or codes of behavior. It is where disobedience is punished. If we set boundaries to help, discipline and keep our children safe, why would we expect God to do less than that? He will not. When we disobey, we exceed the limits that were set for our safety. We enter a danger zone. We sometimes simply travel outside of His will into chaos set by the enemy. As I stated earlier, discipline is practiced and if we practice, we become better in that area.

We need God to change us in any way. I was not going to let the devil continue killing me and the chances my children had for a bright future. Phillip understood my desires. I encouraged him and recognized that he was broken himself. We would just talk for hours and the conversations ranged so greatly. We did not have sex immediately, I would not even go over to his house because I felt the need to go about things differently. He invited me even though I was waiting for the right time. I began going over and never stopped. I was still short on being disciplined though. I knew the things I wanted at the time, but we do not always stay motivated long enough to achieve things.

Our friendship continued to grow. Many areas of our relationship were great, but there were some shady areas that would later be exposed. During the first two years I battled with trusting him. When you do not trust your significant other, you desire a detailed account of everything. He was very patient in the process to restore my trust. What I realized about myself during the process was that I still had unresolved issues with forgiveness anyway. I began to seek God more. I desired a better prayer life. I began to fast. I needed help. I wanted answers.

I prayed many times for God to separate us, disconnect all soul ties, and allow me to move on. I had prayed this prayer in the past in other relationships when I reached the end of my rope. It always worked. This time was different. I could not stop loving him. I could not stop thinking about him. I kept praying, asking God for guidance. Some days I felt so lost. That is how you begin to encounter change. You are stretched beyond your comfort zone into the unknown. In the unknown you cannot rely on what you see but rather trust the Creator who is taking you there. Occasionally, I have stepped out and crossed right back into my comfort zone. You will not experience a radical shift in that position. It does not matter how hard you try. The things that you want, deserve and can achieve will challenge you.

Development is the process for your purpose. God will take all you have experienced and mold you into who you were created to be. Although I thought getting married was not in my future, God knew I was Phillip's wife from the beginning. We do not need to know every detail that lies ahead. The beginning of our relationship taught me two very important things: I learned how to be patient and how to forgive. God was there every step of the way. My submission was a struggle. The Lord desires that we surrender to Him. That struggle would continue up through a few months ago. I was still trying to be in control or control others sometimes. I was not consciously doing it. The lessons can be difficult, but the reward outweighs it.

I was out of work, home and watching the 700 Club. I was laying across the bed and prayed, "God, Phillip asked that I marry him, but how do I know what to do? I need you, Father. If he is my husband, send a sign." I giggled and said, "If he is my husband, I will have a check in the mail today." Considering I was out of work, I thought, *Yeah, that's impossible unless You perform a miracle.* I later drove to check the mailbox, saw an envelope in there and drove off, somehow convinced I was at the wrong mailbox. I then backed up after realizing that it was, in fact, my mailbox. I thought, *Let me check the name on this envelope because it looks like a check.* The check was for over three hundred dollars that was owed to me from the state. Wow! In that moment I began to cry. I was so outdone by the miraculous power of my God. He will provide. He will answer. He will heal. He will deliver. Trust Him! Try Him for yourself!

What I know to be true is that forgiveness brings forth freedom. You will be free to live. Free to love. Free to be at peace. Free to discover your truth. Free from others' negative actions. The purpose of forgiveness is not that you want to ignore that something unfair was done to you; it is to empower you to live free from the anger that accompanies unforgiveness. Recognize it for what it is. If you see someone and it shifts your mood to a negative space or ruins your day, there is some work to be done. Unforgiveness is such a toxic emotion. It slowly kills you.

While you are on your personal journey of life, take the time to explore your truths. If you conclude that you harbor any unresolved emotions, get on track to be healed. The deliverance you need will put you on a path towards your destiny. God knows my life has changed tremendously. I choose to forgive daily. I have no desire to harbor those debilitating emotions. I recognized how great a hold unforgiveness could have on me, so I decided I could forgive easier than hold a grudge. Live your life as a reflection of what you desire to draw in. Do what you do best and that is being you! The very best you. Remember, whom the Son sets free is free indeed!

Tameka Marable King has a powerful message that she shares freely through Facebook, a weekly radio show and her podcast. She and her husband, Phillip are the parents of five children and they work together in ministry. She serves in the media ministry at Six Runs Missionary Baptist Church in Turkey, NC and can be found on all social media outlets as Teeka Talks.

I Choose to Love
Eulanda Thorne

Where do I begin? I have no clue. (Even now), my mind (still) gets weighed down by the thoughts; however, this time around the weight is not a burden to bear. You see, I am reminded of the (powerful) words of my hero, Dr. Maya Angelou; "There's no greater agony than bearing an untold story."

I have a story to tell and I have been bearing the weight of it for far too long. For years, a plethora of thoughts have plagued me. Thoughts about what others might think of my story. Thoughts about what others might say about me. Thoughts which aren't so easy to articulate. Thoughts that run through my mind with no destination. The thoughts have no destination because in my mind, the destination for spoken words is a listening ear. Left unspoken, the words breed that agony which Dr. Maya Angelou spoke of. And when the words run deep, their destination must be approved by God before they are spoken. If you are reading these words, you are hearing your own voice as you read; therefore, your ears have become the destination approved by God for the words of my untold story.

As I share parts of my story, you will begin to see it as more of a journey. I will not share or outline details of my pain, or my struggles. Instead, I will share with you how I got through the difficult times of pain and struggle. In essence, I will share with you "how I got over." And I can tell you right now that I got over through the process of deep, focused, targeted, and intentional *reflecting.* Reflection transforms experiences into genuine learning and the more we learn about ourselves, the greater our capacity to grow; grow from not only trials and pain but life in general.

So, where do I begin? I begin with *you.* If you are reading my words, then you have been chosen by God to assist me in easing the weight of the burden, the heavy thoughts. Sharing my story, even just a part of it, causes the mental suffering to become less. And once the whole story is told, "less" mental suffering will become "alleviated" mental suffering. The more we share our stories, the more connected we feel, the more authentic we become, as we gain more awareness about ourselves. And in this process, through this connection, we give others permission to do the same.

As human beings, we are all connected. Spiritually, we are connected from conception to death. I believe we are connected by our stories of triumph because we all have an area of our life that we have either overcome or are still striving to come out triumphantly. As human beings, I believe we can greatly benefit from self-awareness. I also believe that self-reflection is an important part of who we are and who we aim to be. For this reason, I am an individual who has practiced self-reflection on a regular basis for quite some time. Now that I am an adult, unplanned (single) mom of four, and aspiring toward daily growth in all areas of my life, I have learned that self-reflection will enable me to develop a level of awareness that can assist me in being the best version of myself possible. When I have awareness with understanding of my own life experiences, I believe I can show understanding, empathy, and compassion more effectively towards others. I believe that self-reflection and self-awareness lay a good foundation for me as a human being whose goal truly is "to be the change I wish to see in this world."

So, let's begin! Explore with me as you learn how I got over—through my journey of self-reflection!

Personal Development

Reflecting on my personal development immediately pulls my mind toward my parents. I have inherited their genes that directly relate to who I am. By nature, I am a very sensitive individual. I feel things deeply. While this can be a great attribute (as it has allowed me to be naturally compassionate and empathetic towards others), it has often made me feel as if I am a very weak individual. As a child, not knowing how to use the strong energy that fuels my feelings of empathy and compassion often led me to have feelings of being weak or too soft in a world where others a more emotionally strong.

I began to have feelings of being depressed that later manifested into actual symptoms of depression. Many years later, I ended up being diagnosed with depression and later auto-immune disease, that could possibly be attributed to not understanding (or failure to accept) who I was. After the diagnosis (which I did not want to accept), it did not take long for me to learn that my mother had also suffered from depression off and on throughout her life. She often shared with me that I was manifesting symptoms of depression around the same age she did and that I was indeed depressed. I later believed that perhaps the *main* reason for my initial "feelings" of being depressed was because of my mother's perception of my behaviors as related to my extreme sensitivity. It is unfortunate that my emotional sensitivity and *perceived* bouts with depression became the area of focus when defining myself. Once I was able to overcome those false perceptions, I knew I would be able to see myself in the true light of all my greatness.

Where it All Began

My mother had me and married my father when she was 18 years old. (She had my brother at 16.) My dad was 21 when I was born. Although both my parents had finished high school when I was born, they were very young and had begun serious dating at an early age. Both my parents came from large families. My mother is the oldest of 11 children and my dad has 7 other siblings. These facts, coupled with marrying young, made them both feel the pressures of leaving their families and almost immediately creating and starting their own. There was no time of being independent. This was both a blessing and a curse. The blessing was that my parents understood the importance of family and have always valued family tremendously. However, there was no time between leaving home and marriage during which they could grow and mature as individuals. The result was they fought a lot. During my childhood, I remember lots of fussing and fighting between my parents. Perhaps, they were not as mature or stable as they should have been before having kids and marrying. Looking on the bright side, (reflecting in ways to foster growth), my parents grew *together*. They built *together*. They have been solid together (and just celebrated 46 years of marriage). Despite the arguing, there was a very strong sense of love, family, and the desire to make things work. Later, you will learn how this fact contributed to me staying in an abusive marriage for 13 years; I was trying to make things work as my parents did.

I grew up in the '70s. During that time, my parents' socio-economic status was considered poor. Neither had college degrees. My dad did factory work and my mom worked off and on. Although I grew up in a home with little financially, I can honestly say that I never (not even once) felt as if we were poor. During my early elementary school years, I can remember having only one pair of denim jeans and only one pair of tennis shoes (sneakers); however, my dad worked very hard to provide for us. By the time I was seven years old, my dad had a good paying factory job. Financially, things became better. My mother became a foster parent (for over 10 years), so I grew up with other children in our home who were even less fortunate than my brother and me. This taught me so much about empathy, compassion, and selflessness. By the time I was in high school, I had a pretty good sense of self (although I had some insecurities) and I was very popular mostly due to my great character. Other than the fact that I grew up extremely sheltered, I can't think of any *possible* regrets about my childhood. Overall, what I remember most about my childhood is that my dad always provided for us, and we had a safe home filled with love. I was taught the importance of getting a good education, having a good work ethic and working hard. I was taught the importance of family and I was raised with excellent morals and values. I believe not having much materialistically but having a magnitude of struggles paired with love and good morals has greatly contributed to who I am today.

    As a child, I watched my dad struggle through very difficult jobs which were extremely taxing on his body. On top of this, he very seldom took time out for himself. In the end, he feels he has been rewarded as he has now retired with several streams of income. The experiences my dad modeled before me have conditioned me to believe that I too will be rewarded if I work hard (for someone else as he did with factory jobs) and can enjoy my retirement in the end. Even now, I am verbally praised (rewarded) by my dad when he sees me working hard, attending graduate school, working two jobs, and providing for my children as a single mom. At times, I have felt like he was rewarding me for pushing my body too hard and for denying myself the outlet and breaks that I need to be healthy and whole.

Because my mom had my brother and me at a young age and married at a young age, she felt "tied down" and deprived of her youth. On the other hand, I married at age 27 and had my four children afterwards. Unintentionally, I had learned from my mom that after getting married and having children, my life was over. (This is something she has said often). I later understood that this operant conditioning in my mind is what caused me to totally lose myself in my marriage. I lost a good concept of who I was and became known (to myself) as a wife and a mother, nothing more. I had dismissed that I was also an individual who loved to travel, someone who enjoyed adventure and exploring, and someone who enjoyed meeting new people. I was praised as a good wife and mom, for denying myself, and being consumed with those wife/mom duties. Even through the pain, not having an outlet, and literally almost having a nervous breakdown, I still had not learned that I must make time for myself. The fact that I would not be as effective for anyone else if I didn't first take care of my own needs was not in the forefront of my mind. The perceived "good sense of self" came into question during my adult life.

Adulting & Marriage

I was married to the father of my four children for 13 years. During those 13 years, there was lots of infidelity (on his part) along with verbal, mental and emotional abuse disguised as love. My children's father was very manipulative and deceptive. On the other hand, I was very naive, forgiving, and had a very pure heart. Because he and I had personalities on totally opposite ends of the spectrum, his narcissism left me severely scared and insecure. Reflecting on the facts earlier, I was also very sensitive. During my marriage, I began seeing my sensitive nature as a weakness and I was also being emotionally neglected in my marriage.

My ex-husband had a deeply-rooted sexual addiction and I married him as a virgin at 27 years old. In my naivety, I thought having a sexual addiction meant that one simply enjoyed sex and enjoyed having it more often than most. I couldn't have been more wrong. The symptoms and manifestations of his addiction ranged from watching pornography excessively, pathological lying, severe manipulation, sexually transmitted disease, even wiping out our bank account, visiting strip clubs during a time when not only were we both unemployed, but I was home with an 18-month-old child and a newborn. Needless to say, two more kids later, and 13 years into the marriage (yes, 13 years), I finally gained the strength and courage to leave the bondage that was disguised as a marriage. Before leaving, I had nearly lost my mind (literally) and I had unquestionably lost my sense of self-worth. After all, I thought I was simply pleasing God (as told to me by my ex-husband) by being the "submissive wife." Unfortunately, I was left severely mentally and emotionally scarred and it would take years later before I realized the depth of the emotional, mental and psychological abuse I had suffered (and unconsciously embraced as acceptable) during those 13 years.

The Shift

In 2011, I began a search to understand where the depth of my insecurities stemmed from when prior to this point in my life, I'd always had a decent concept of my self-worth. Because I had always been the most sensitive child in my family, the one who literally wanted to save the world and have world peace, the one who would regularly give her lunch money away and go without eating so that someone else could eat, the one who would forgive the most unfathomable offenses, someone who was easily taken advantage of because of such a pure heart etc., because of these behaviors my family members gave me a nickname. In my family, I was often called the "Dumb Blonde" of the family. (And because blondes are usually Caucasian, and I am African American, the color "black" was often inserted before saying "dumb blonde.") It wasn't until 2012 that I realized how severely scarred I had become from that family nickname. I honestly do not feel my family meant any harm by calling me a dumb blonde; however, they had labeled me. I had come to believe that because I was a sensitive individual who saw the best in everyone, I was indeed "dumb."

In January of 2012, I had returned from Tucson, Arizona where I had attended an educational conference. The founder of this conference, (renowned psychologist, Howard Glasser) returned with us to do a training at our school. God would have it so that Mr. Glasser saw something beyond great, marvelous, and life-changing in me that I (up until that point) was not able to see in myself. He and I were standing in the doorway of my principal's office and he was "telling me about my greatness." In return, I began inadvertently refuting all the greatness that he saw in me. I remember telling him my entire "Dumb Blonde" story and how because of that, I have always thought that something was *wrong* with my personality and that I was *flawed*. It was at that moment, immediately after I spoke those words, that Mr. Glasser grabbed both of my hands, looked me directly in my eyes and spoke these life-changing words to me (literally life-changing), "Eulanda my dear, nothing about you is flawed. I am literally mesmerized when I watch you teach your students. You're not flawed at all. In fact, you're just the opposite; you're flawless! Your perceived flaws are what make you great.

They're your fuel. They're what make you stand out. They're what make you unique. They're what make you who you are. Those traits of sensitivity, trusting, vulnerability, forgiving... they are not flaws at all. They're your superpowers!" I don't believe Mr. Glasser even recognized that he was being used by God to speak into my life. That encounter was the beginning of my life being forever changed. I no longer had to define myself as the dumb blonde others said I was.

Sealing It

The painful experiences surrounding my divorce and the judgments my family made about me (being a dumb blonde) both go hand-in-hand. I had created my self-image based on the comments and beliefs of others. Believing I was weak, and the cause of my failed marriage greatly scarred me. But something happened one day, and it was by no goodness of my own. God's grace, mercy and love for me overpowered my self-doubt. I think it was because I desperately wanted to be healed and to greatly benefit the world. When I was a young girl, I made a vow to God that I would give the world the best I had; although, it may never be enough. Remembering that I asked God to make me an instrument of His love... and that I would *love* others, *serve* others and *give* with no conditions attached.

Reminding myself today of this belief, I believe if I keep searching for everything beautiful in this world, I will eventually become it. I must continue to *be* the change I wish to see in this world. I know that anyone can find the dirt in someone, but I consciously choose to be the one who finds the gold. You see, no matter how messed up we may think we are, there will always be someone who loves us and still thinks we're amazing! In the end, I made a vow to myself to always choose love because in the end, love always wins. Not only does loving ourselves bring healing but loving others does the same. I consciously chose to never allow my heart to become bitter even when I was hurt loving others. When we're going through emotionally and/or mentally painful experiences, we have a choice. We can consciously choose to "reset" to a deeper place of love, or bitterness.

When we reset to love, we're allowing our heart to jump start, almost likened to defibrillation of the heart. During this process a brief electric shock is given to the heart to reset the heart back to its normal rhythm. If the heart isn't reset, one's heart could literally stop beating (stop loving) permanently resulting in death of the heart (death of the capacity to forgive, believe, trust and love). Don't stop being who you are. Don't stop being true to your truths. But don't stop loving either. Whatever your greatness is, whatever your super power is, *don't you dare* allow it to be stifled because of hurt, pain, or unforgiveness. Keep being your unique self. Keep being you. Because You Are Amazing just the way you are!

Remember the song, "Encourage Yourself?" Well, the majority of the time when I write, it is for me. However, I know the things I write can also be uplifting to others. So in this moment as I write, perhaps my writing will bring clarity, strength or encouragement to someone. If you're having a moment of feeling worn down by the things of this world, feeling alone, frustrated, or confused, just remind yourself of all your greatness and beauty. And if you're not yet at that place where you can see your greatness or beauty, that's okay too. Just remember that you truly do have a "choice" in the matter. Yep. Today, and every day, we all have choices to make from the time we open our eyes and begin our day.

Years ago, (and even now) I chose to use the fuel from an insurmountable amount of pain to rebuild myself. I wanted to be better not bitter. I wanted to be stronger not weaker. I wanted to be wiser not naïve or foolish. I wanted to be more loving and more forgiving, not full of hate or revenge. I have learned that although pain is inevitable, there are two ways you can go with pain. You can let it destroy you or you can use it as fuel to drive you towards great love, greater understanding with empathy and compassion for others. Even those who may have harmed you. I've learned that I must embrace pain and use it as fuel to propel me forward on my journey towards my destiny and sharing the greatness that lives within me! Use the pain as a reminder of my strength. So, I have been conditioned and learned to *embrace* my journey. Today, and every day, I choose forgiveness. I choose compassion. I choose empathy. I choose love. Every. Single. Time. It isn't always easy but is it most definitely always worth it!

I'm reminding myself today that I am enough. I'm reminding myself today that I, (more than anyone else) am deserving of my own love. I'm reminding myself today that I do matter, and I am loved. I'm reminding myself today that yes, I am romantic about the little things in life and that's okay because I appreciate life and all things in it. I'm reminding myself today that I am an individual who is passionate, and I feel deeply and that is okay. I'm reminding myself today that (although I will make mistakes along the way) I am doing an amazing job in life. I'm reminding myself today that I am a loving mother. I'm reminding myself today that I am a wonderful daughter, an amazing friend, a great sister, a loving teacher, and an empathetic counselor. Sensitivity, empathy, and compassion. These are my superpowers.

An Overcomer!

So, how do *I* see myself? I absolutely love the woman I have become. I have fought hard to become her! I embrace all my strengths and I use the energy of my weaknesses to propel me forward toward more strength and greatness! I focus on how strong I've become and all the wisdom I have gained because of life's experiences. I am a strong and intelligent woman whose capacity for forgiveness, compassion, and empathy makes me a uniquely beautiful woman full of love. I bear my own struggles and experiences, pulling from the strength of my upbringing and my heritage. I appreciate, own, and accept all my experiences for they made me the beautiful woman I am today! I now see myself as a gift to this world. Every so often, I find it "needful" to speak a healthy self-love affirmation to myself. I'm teaching my children the same. As I write now, my affirmation speaks:

I am beautiful. My inner beauty shines outwardly. I love and approve of myself. I see, acknowledge, and appreciate my growth. I'm thankful for my resiliency as I continue to embrace my journey. As I accept myself, I am free from the burden of needing others to accept me. Though it is a process, I celebrate my conscious decision to release my past pain and live only in the present. This way, I get to enjoy and experience life to the fullest as God intends for me (and my children). I am my own version of beautiful which no one else can be. I boldly and confidently say, "Eulanda, I love you and I'm so proud of you!"

I'm still on my journey toward wholeness and God is not finished with me. A journey of intentional and purposeful self-reflection can be powerful beyond measure *if* we're honest and open with ourselves and with God. Through this journey of self-reflection, *This* is how I got over!

Eulanda Thorne, a public school counselor and Nurtured Heart consultant is passionate about living a life that pleases God. She is the mother of four children and she resides in Wilson, NC.

From Rejected to Redeemed
Iris Peterson Bryant

"You are a Cabbage Patch Kid!"
"*They* are not your *real* parents!"
"My grandmother said that you are adopted!"
"At least I know who my *real* parents are!"

When I was growing up, these words became the anthem that was heralded around me. During my earliest years of school, I learned quickly that the "appropriate" way to retaliate was with the popular phrase, "Sticks and stones may break my bones, but words will never hurt me!" That was my automatic response, and I would proclaim it with much conviction, but internally I was not convinced that truth was embedded in the words I spoke. If these words I heard on the playground, school bus, at family gatherings and even at church could never hurt me, why did I have to nurse the wounds and the mental "after effects" later? If these words could never hurt me, why did I feel like my heart was bleeding?

The truth is, these words did not leave any visible signs of pain—except on the days these words led to physical altercations—but the pain these words inflicted upon my spirit lasted decades.

My third grade teacher was the first of many adults I sought for refuge when my elementary school classmates began their customary playground taunts about the subject of adoption. The first time I spoke with Mrs. Lucas was on a Monday morning after a letter circulated in our choir the night before.

During our church's missionary service, our youth choir

would provide music. On this particular Sunday night as during most church services, I was sitting beside my dad, who also served as the youth choir advisor. Most people knew I sat beside him because I was a "daddy's girl," but they were not aware that he also kept me beside him to guarantee I did not misbehave during the services. With him as my neighbor I was careful to do the right thing—which meant no gum chewing, no talking, and absolutely no note-passing in church.

While sitting in the choir I noticed a note being passed from one choir member to another. I heard the rustling of paper and the giggles of my friends and cousins. I could hardly wait until the note reached my row, and I even devised a plan, so I wouldn't actually pass the note, but I could still read it. Once the note landed in the hands of the neighbor to my right, I would read it out of the corner of my eye and never have to accept the note into my hands. This scheme would automatically protect me from my neighbor to my left—my dad! I knew by the whispers that the note was a definite "hot topic."

Would the note reveal someone's "church crush?" Would it be the latest school gossip? Could it be a note about someone in church?

My mind was flooded with countless scenarios and I was anticipating this information would be a great conversation piece during our ride to school the next day. I watched as the note was passed to everyone, and just as I planned when the note finally reached my neighbor, I glanced over to read, "Do not let Iris read this. Iris is a Cabbage Patch Kid."

It seemed that time stood still, and the rest of the church service progressed in slow motion as I read and reread the words then stored them in my personal mental notebook.

Cabbage Patch Kids were very popular during this time of my childhood and the fact that they were advertised as "one of a kind" was not the quality that stood out to me. I understood without a doubt they were alluding to adoption.

As my family and I rode home that night, I asked a question and a *holy hush* fell like a cloud in the '77 Buick my dad was driving.

"Am I adopted?"

I had neither the tact nor the understanding of the right timing, but I was wise enough to know that something was being spoken before Mom or Daddy said a single word. Years later, I would have understood how to interpret their silence, but that night I only understood they were shocked by my question.

My mom broke the silence by calmly stating, "Iris, we are all adopted into God's family."

I was momentarily appeased, but deep down inside there was something telling me the note was not someone's mean, jealous opinion, but it was a fact. My question was not answered directly.

I wanted to know the truth, *maybe.*

The next day at school I talked to Mrs. Lucas and she gave me a laundry list of reasons why children made fun of other children. I was able to see Mrs. Lucas as a teacher who was not only determined to help me as I struggled with multiplication facts but also as someone who truly cared about me. During that tumultuous school year, I was determined that whether I was adopted or not, I was definitely going to be a teacher.

Several months later, I decided to surprise my parents by giving them a gift that was given to me. I had received a U.S. Savings Bond and wanted to contribute it to our yearly family vacation. At that moment, the idea of getting the key and unlocking the family trunk to retrieve the bond seemed like a harmless gesture, but what I would learn is the key gave me access to much more than a $25.00 Savings bond. The key unlocked a plethora of facts that had been concealed in one document.

Prior to entering kindergarten, I was taught to spell my

name I-r-i-s-h, but upon entering kindergarten, I began spelling my name without the "h." When I saw the legal size envelope with "Irish Larue Peterson" written on it, I knew I had found the right papers. When I opened the envelope I realized that I had not found the savings bond for which I was searching, but I had found adoption papers that I had been convinced did not exist.

I waited until my two younger siblings were put to bed before I told my parents I had a problem I needed to talk to them about. When we met in the living room I arrived with tears in my eyes and the adoption papers in my hand.

I cried. My dad cried. My mom just kept repeating that she was so relieved.

At the time I was too young to understand it all, but I sat and listened to my parents talk about their desire to have children and the fact that they believed God had chosen them to be my parents. I was not born to them, but they chose me. I went to bed that night feeling more special than I had ever felt in my life.

I was old enough to know that the words in that note were factual; I was indeed a Cabbage Patch Kid by definition, but I was also loved beyond measure.

Although I was able to receive the love from my parents and understand their actions, as well as their purposeful and successful attempts to help me fit in, I still struggled with the issue of my adoption. On the night I found my papers, my parents said to me, "We are your mom and dad, you are our daughter, and nothing will ever change that." I believed them, but I also believed that if I asked them any questions concerning my adoption, I would be disrespecting them and dishonoring the sacrifices they made for me.

However, if I was ever idle or upset, overwhelming thoughts and questions would flood my mind.

"Was I given up for adoption because I was bald as a baby?"
"Did I cry too much as an infant?"

"Was my birth mother too young to care for me?"
"Was she afraid?"
"Did she wonder where I was?"
"Did she have ponies and a swimming pool?"
"Was she a rich lady who lived in a mansion?"

The questions flowed like a raging river in my brain. I would glimpse passing automobiles that I was not familiar with and imagine she was riding by to check on me. I imagined that she spent sleepless nights regretting her decision to give me up for adoption.

One day while visiting the home of one my maternal aunts, I asked her and her children if they knew I was adopted. They were completely caught off guard with my random question, but they were never a family to be at a loss for words.

Her youngest daughter, Theresa, who was about 8 years older than me said, "Girl, yeah, we know you are adopted, and I am your mama!"

The entire house erupted into laughter and her quick, snide remark made me realize that I would always be wanted!

I had never been taunted by any of my relatives on my mother's side of the family and it was at that instant I realized family was not about who gave birth to you, it was about who loved you unconditionally. My cousin Theresa is known for being a jokester and always making sure others are laughing, but that day, the message conveyed to me was deeper than the words she spoke.

Yes, others knew I was adopted but that didn't change our relationship. We had a connection that transcended bloodlines. It reminded me of my mother's words, "We are all adopted into God's family."

His love for His children reaches beyond family lines and any other commonalities and as a result of our relationship with Him and His great love for us, we can call others our family.

That summer day in my aunt's house, laughter and a joke

tore down a wall I had erected in my life. In the back of my mind, I had believed I was tolerated but not accepted. I believed everyone was being nice to me because it was the right thing to do. It was the enemy's plan to convince me I was not loved as a cousin but as an *adopted* cousin. I overcame that idea because it was evident that I was loved. Plain and simple, loved and accepted.

I embraced that new revelation and decided on that day I would not allow the fact that I was adopted to hinder me from accepting love from my family, who freely offered this unconditional love with no reservations.

I believed that inwardly there was a war raging to steal my peace. If I became absorbed with what I thought others felt about me, I would not be free to accept their unconditional love. I began to remove the walls from my mind and wholeheartedly fell in love with a huge group of aunts, uncles and cousins who had fallen in love with me on the day I entered their lives.

Just as the word of God must fall on good ground in order to produce a great harvest, so shall the words we believe about ourselves. The day I decided to move forward was the day the enemy began to set up an ambush in my mind and subtly convince me that although I was loved by many, there were others who did not love me.

I was reminded that somewhere someone had made a decision to carry me for nine months but not for a lifetime. The joy of being accepted by one family was not enough because I was reminded that another family had rejected me. This war was waged to prevent me from moving forward into a place of inner peace.

One family tradition that was instituted by my dad was our yearly, out-of-state vacation. Our vacation always occurred during his birthday week, the last week in August. We would alternate each year between family visits and amusement parks or historical locations.

Special memories were created during these vacations; although, as children we only saw the fun of the road trips to various states along the eastern seaboard.

When we traveled to amusement parks, I was overwhelmed by the fact that we were five people from a small town in North Carolina in a sea of hundreds of thousands of people from all over the world. People from all walks of life and different parts of the world had passed through the entrance of the park gates. I would gaze into the eyes of the people, wondering if it was possible that I was staring into the eyes of a biological family member. Was it possible that one of those faces in the masses belonged to me?

What I felt I was missing was a sense of belonging. The most striking definition of the word belong is, *"to have the proper qualifications, especially social qualifications, to be a member of a group."* In our society, so many people just want to be connected to something greater.

The enemy was defeated when I embraced the love given by my family, but he crept back in and planted a seed in the seat of my emotions. The inner whispers that mocked me, convinced me that although my family loved me, I would never truly *belong* to them.

One year while visiting relatives in New Jersey, we went on an excursion to Asbury Park for an evening of fun. I remember engaging in a long stare at a woman who was placing an order at a nearby concession stand. As I gazed at this beautiful woman, I had time to process a multitude of thoughts.

Was my birth mom as beautiful as this woman?

Did my birth mom find joy in ordering a sausage dog with onions for my younger siblings, who I believed existed somewhere out there?

This lady was indeed beautiful on the outside, but when she saw me staring, she turned to see if my eyes were glaring a hole into someone else's skin. Realizing that she was the object of my attention, she then turned back and voiced a few expletives that would have made Richard Pryor blush. My reverie was broken as well as my belief that the person I belonged to was looking for me.

I spent most of my teen years going back and forth about finding my birth mother. I often questioned if she "deserved" to have a relationship with me. I wondered if I would ever know and understand the circumstances that led her to make the decision not to keep me.

I graduated high school, attended college and received a degree in English Education. I was determined I was going to make an impact in the lives of young people. Aside from my parents, many of my teachers had been the most influential people in my life and I felt compelled to extend that same inspiration to the next generation.

I loved my job as a teacher and the unexplainable joy that came with the job. I did not mind the long hours and seemingly low pay because I believed I was making a direct impact on the future.

Every time I reached a milestone or made a major accomplishment in life, I wondered if the time was finally right for me to search for my birth family. I had a deep love and respect for my parents and it was my deepest fear that I would be exhibiting ungratefulness for all they had done for me.

Several of my life-long friends became confidants as they listened to me waver over the decision to look for my birth mother. I made and broke pacts with each of them concerning that pursuit. I promised we could look for her when I turned 18, but I changed my mind the week before my 18th birthday. I promised to look when I turned 21, but I broke that promise to them as well. Seeing the unreliability of their friend, they started initiating the conversation and offered a resolution to my questions.

"Let's write Dear Abby," was the request of one friend.

Another friend suggested hiring a private investigator. Someone else decided we should go directly to the source of the adoption—the Department of Social Services. Respectfully, I declined their offers and resolved if it was meant for me to find my birth family, God would have to orchestrate it. I don't know why I had not made that decision earlier because it seemed like the only rational decision to make. I imagined all of the horrible scenarios that could occur if I tried to seek out my birth family on my own. I had to believe if God did the work, then the outcome would be favorable for all involved.

My closest friends listened to my decision and I informed them we would only talk about the subject of adoption if I brought it up. I remember the looks of confusion and grave concern they displayed as I outlined this new rule. They all agreed, in spite of their unspoken reservations.

Years later I found myself in a situation that once again made me cry out to God for direction about my adoption. I was expecting my first child and staring down at a medical chart that had always been a source of contention for me, the part of the form that required information about my medical background. I submitted the forms without completing the information, but when I left the office, I was prompted to visit the Department of Social Services (DSS) in the county where I was adopted and request non-identifying medical information. They were unable to provide the requested information and instructed me to visit the county where I was born. I was able to speak to the departmental supervisor who listened as I provided the date of my birth, date of adoption, the county of adoption and even the name of the lawyer who finalized the adoption. There was no record! I walked out of the DSS office and felt a horrible sensation in the pit of my stomach. I was in a state of sheer frustration. I sat outside the office and wept as my mind replayed a moment from an earlier disappointment in my life.

I remembered the embarrassment I felt as a high school student involved in a program called Economics in Action. We'd spent an entire day visiting our local government officials and getting a glimpse of a day in their lives. I was with a group of five or six other students as we visited the records room with the Register of Deeds. Our task was to find our birth certificates in the records room, so we could get a copy to take home with us. I was accompanied by the clerk during my search, but we could not find my birth certificate.

She stated as professionally as she could, "There are only two reasons you wouldn't have a birth certificate on file: you were born in another county, or you were adopted."

Needless to say, being professional does not lessen the humiliation of being embarrassed in the presence of your peers. We still had several other officials to visit, but I knew that visit to the courthouse would be my least favorite stop.

So now, more than a decade later, I was hit with that same uneasy, gnawing feeling. I could not go to the county courthouse and get a birth certificate like most people because I was adopted. Here I was seeking something I had a legal right to receive, non-identifying information, and I could not access that. I knew I was alive and breathing, but because there were tangible public records that did not exist, I began to feel the same way about myself.

"God, please heal me," was my new prayer.

A few months later my son was born. When I saw him, my heart melted—it was indeed love at first sight. I was still very lethargic from the anesthesia that was required during my emergency cesarean section, but when I touched his little hands and rubbed his arms, I knew for the first time that I could recall, I was actually touching someone who was a part of me. An overwhelming sense of peace and the presence of God consumed me. I cried tears that were interpreted as tears of joy by the onlookers in the NICU, but those tears were tears of release from years of bondage. I was touching someone who was connected to me. This was my son, my baby, my child and he looked like me—he was mine. Finally I was connected to another person on earth. I was blessed with a child.

Twenty-one months later, I gave birth to a beautiful daughter, who was sugar and spice and everything nice. I was granted eight weeks of maternity leave and enjoyed my time at home with her. However one day while feeding her, it dawned on me that she was the exact same age I was when I was placed for adoption. My salty tears fell on her precious six-week-old face as I wondered what it must have felt like to leave behind a little girl identical to the one I was holding. A steady stream of emotions overshadowed me: anger, rage, unbelief, pain, fear and grief forced me to gasp for breath. I sat in the house alone and afraid.

Although I was fulfilled as a mother, there was still an ache in my heart. Actually, to say my soul ached would be an understatement.

Should I continue living with unanswered questions or should I obey my heart's desire and seek answers? These thoughts would always race to my mind at the most inopportune times. However, I will never forget that day in May 2008 when I felt my world shift forever. I was sensing that God was calling me on a fast. I was experiencing a tumultuous season in my life and had been praying in preparation for the fast—asking God for healing from the pain of my past and clarity for the days ahead.

One night during the fast, I was traveling with four of my friends after an out of town church service. We'd had an awesome experience in worship that evening and continued to enjoy each other's company as we traveled home that night. We had been riding for less than fifteen minutes when one of the women in the van began to lament concerning her struggles raising an adopted child. She startled me by relaying the message she had shared with her husband earlier.

"Iris would never put her parents through the things that our child has put us through."

That one sentence transformed me back to the day I wrote on my baby brother's crib because of jealousy. His birth had changed my status from only child to big sister. I began to view my childhood on a mental jumbotron. How much trouble had I caused for my parents when I made foolish decisions in relationships, when I dropped out of college because I felt defeated? Was I the subject of late night conversations as my parents recapped the negative events of the day? Did they ever feel like I was causing undue stress for them? Did they ever regret adopting me?

As we continued traveling home that night, my silence became increasingly noticeable. Someone asked if I was okay and I responded, very tersely, that I was far from okay. I began to unleash a myriad of raw emotions. Uncertainty, pain, anger and fear were prominent. For the first time, I was not afraid or ashamed of revealing my vulnerabilities concerning the topic of adoption. I was so consumed and aware of the thoughts racing through my mind, that it did not matter whether I was speaking gibberish or not—I was finally free to speak my thoughts. I was able to say, for the first time, that my issues with rejection and the need to belong stemmed from a deep longing to be accepted by a person I did not know. I had questions and I needed answers.

"How do you want me to pray?" one of the ladies asked.

"I am so scared. What if I am rejected again?"

"You won't be rejected. How do you want me to pray? You

have two options tonight: we can pray that God will heal you through meeting them, or we can pray that He will heal you without meeting them. But whatever you pray, you must believe that tonight is the last night you will be tortured by the subject of adoption. What do you want?"

After silent meditation, with tears in my eyes, I simply said, "I want to know."

An earnest prayer was offered and at the conclusion, my covenant sisters agreed.

"Amen," I whispered. Let it be so.

In that moment supernatural peace came over me. A peace unlike anything I had ever experienced before. I was overshadowed with the peace and presence of God and I knew without a doubt He heard the prayer and an answer would be forthcoming.

Knowing some things only occur through fasting and praying, I continued the fast, knowing God was going to heal me and make me whole.

Eight months later, while completing household chores, my daughter began crying and complaining about all of the work she had to do. She sounded just like her mommy as a child. As I worked in my bedroom across the hall, I listened to her utter the same things I had uttered growing up. I remembered being punished on many occasions for not keeping my room clean. I walked into my son's room and saw he was as busy as a bee and seemed to enjoy putting his toys and clothes in their proper places.

With tears in my eyes, I walked into my daughter's room and talked to her. I heard what she said with my ears, but I felt what she said in my heart.

God, I prayed in my heart, *don't allow the bad part of me to become a bad part of her.*

The *bad* part of me? What was that and where did it come

from? The *bad* part of me... That day I was filled with an unbearable sense of sadness. As I knelt to pray before bed, I offered the most ridiculous prayer to a Father Who knows all things.

Have you ever been afraid to pray? I don't mean the 'I am so unworthy' pity party that the enemy attempts to launch our way, but a deeply embedded fear that God just might answer your prayer?

"Dear Lord, You know what I am going to ask, but tonight, Lord, I am not ready to ask. I am afraid of what you might show me. Help me, please. Amen."

Fear had never hindered me from praying on behalf of others. If someone else asked me to pray for them, I didn't hesitate, and I prayed with confidence. I knew God would honor the request of anything asked in His will. Why could I believe that others would receive an answered prayer, but doubt He would hear and answer my heart's cry?

I fell asleep as the tears soaked my pillow.

The next day I asked for help in being free to make my petition known to God. As I knelt down that night to pray, I spoke again from my heart and asked God to reveal to me what He wanted me to know about my past in order that my daughter would not experience the same things I had experienced in life. I wanted to be free, so I could model freedom for her. I wanted to be whole, so she would never have to wonder what wholeness was.

I continued to pour out the locked contents of my heart to my Father. As I asked Him to prick my birth mother's heart so that she would accept me and give me peace and direction for locating her, I felt a tremendous weight lift from my shoulders.

After I had emptied out my heart to the Lord, I went to sleep, and it was while I was sleeping, that God began answering my prayers.

I have had a belief for many years that God unlocks and reveals important messages to His children while they sleep, but I did not understand the magnitude of this level of revelation until days later. As I slept, God whispered in the night.

I was in our church and a minister stood and asked us to find a specific name in the Bible. The task was daunting, and I kept uttering, "That name is not in the Bible." I was astonished as I looked around at several people who were finding the name. They stood with their Bibles and walked out of the sanctuary smiling. The more I searched for the name, the more frustrated I became. I stood to walk out when one of the greeters at our church, Ms. Annie Mae, said she would help me. I sat down beside her, and we searched the scriptures for that particular name. We stood on Isaiah 43. I jumped up in excitement and ran out of the sanctuary to show the minister I had found the scripture. He took me to a completely different place in the sanctuary and instructed me to look around at what God wanted to show me. As I looked around, everything seemed heavenly. It was the most beautiful sight I had ever seen. He told me that everything was being made new.

I awoke on Monday morning, headed to work and carried out my normal duties and responsibilities. I considered the dream throughout the day, but I never paused to consider the words found in Isaiah 43 nor did it dawn on me that the dream was indeed a message from God.

When I arose on Tuesday, it seemed as if someone had flipped on the light switch of my mind. I could not move forward until I read the words of Isaiah 43. I sat and stared at the first verse, reading it over and over again.

"But now thus saith the LORD that created thee, O Jacob, and he that formed thee, O Israel, Fear not: for I have redeemed thee, I have called thee by thy name; thou art mine."

Each time I read it, I substituted Jacob and Israel with my name. God formed me, and He knew everything about me. I began to look at the intricate details of the dream and I knew without a doubt that God had sent an answer. He only gave me the dream when I was in a place where I could handle it. I believed that if he brought me to it, then He was more than capable of bringing me through it. *Here we go, Jesus; I trust You with my whole life.*

As a youngster, I was tortured by nightmares and I was constantly overwhelmed with fear. There were many nights when I awoke in tears because of various dreams that terrified me. For several weeks I dreamed about two women chasing me. They would run behind me as if to capture me and I would try to get away from them. I would cry out in fear and my mom would come into my room and lay in bed with me until I drifted back to sleep. There would be nights when I would fall asleep listening to her pray for me.

Years later, I would come to understand the enemy had planted terror and fear in my heart by invading my dreams. The same method the enemy used to terrorize me as a child would be the instrument God would use to deliver a message to me to alter the course of my life. I believed that even if I never had the opportunity to meet my birth mother, I could still rest in the knowledge that I had been redeemed by a loving Savior. That message resonated loudly and clearly in my heart.

Over the next two days I had analyzed every aspect of the dream and was ready to do what had to be done to "walk it out." Thursday night I prayed before I called Ms. Annie Mae. When she answered the phone, I didn't waste any time—I got straight to the point.

She and I had attended the same church for years but had never had a phone conversation prior to that Thursday evening. When I called her she was surprised, and I know her facial expression must have changed dramatically as I went through my spiel without pausing to breathe.

"Do you know anyone who lives in Duplin County who may have given birth to a baby girl in October of 1973 and given her up for adoption?"

Slowly, she asked me to repeat my question.

I hesitated to say it all again. I wondered if she was of the school of thought that believed in sweeping things under the rug. Would she blame me for bringing up a dead issue? Would she believe in keeping secrets and protecting secret-creators?

I had made it this far. I worked up the nerve to ask her about the baby girl born in October 1973 once again. This time I also shared my dream. At the culmination of my conversation, I boldly asked if she could help me.

"Ms. Annie Mae, you helped me in my dream. You guided me to the answer and I truly believe you can help me now."

She began to stutter, "Iris, this is a lot. I will have to wait until Monday to do anything because I am going to need the weekend to get myself together. I will call you next week."

We said good-bye and I felt relieved that I had made the phone call. The awesome thing about completing an assignment is the peace that follows. I was not anxious or nervous or confused when I ended the phone call. I was completely content, and my mind did not even race ahead to Monday. I went to bed in peace and awoke knowing that God was in control.

While attending intercessory prayer at our church two days following our phone conversation, I was surprised to see Ms. Annie Mae become so emotional when I walked past her as I exited the sanctuary. She followed me into the vestibule and explained the reason for her tears.

"I have never seen you wear your hair like that, and when you walked past me, I saw a vision of a lady who has to be your mother. I believe your birth mother and I attended school together. I felt like I knew she was your birth mother when you called me the other night, but I wasn't sure until I saw you today."

I knew I was still draped in a cloak of supernatural peace because although I watched her wipe tears from her eyes, inwardly I was content to rest in God and trust Him to carry this out in His own way. I went home and put the conversation out of my mind. Later that night, while eating at a local pizza restaurant, I realized I had missed a call from Ms. Annie Mae.

Pushing my salad plate aside, with shaky fingers I dialed her number. There was no formal greeting or wasted words when she answered the phone.

"I just saw your mother and she wants to meet you," said the voice from the other end of the line.

I started screaming and crying in the restaurant and drew the attention of all those around me. Trying not to further interrupt anyone's night with my good news, I raced outside to speak to her in private.

"Your mother is a beautiful woman and you have three brothers and a big family that will probably be so glad to get a chance to meet you." She was rambling on in the same fashion I had just a few days earlier.

Needless to say, my appetite was gone, and I was on cloud nine! The joy I felt was indescribable and I knew it only came because I trusted God's way and His timing.

I had four days of preparation before I went to meet my birth mother.

As the day approached, I once again experienced every emotion imaginable. I had dreamed of the day we would finally meet, and I envisioned her running toward me in slow motion, just as I had seen in the reunion of Nettie and her children from the movie adaptation of Alice Walker's *The Color Purple*. I had rehearsed what she would say when we met, which would lead to me shedding tears of joy. I imagined her stroking my face, as a mother would stroke the face of a newborn child.

It is funny how the media can distort our view of reality.

We met in a safe, private setting, and when she walked into the room, neither of us ran toward the other. I had been told she was a beautiful woman and that I looked like her, but when she walked into the room, the first thing I realized was that we were dressed alike. I was taken aback immediately.

Black shoes, black pants, an aqua shell and black coat was her attire. Her outfit was accessorized with a silver necklace with a circular pendant. I wore black shoes, black pants, and a black shell with an aqua blouse. My accessory was a silver necklace with an oval pendant. I was in shock that we were actually dressed alike. Would there be any other similarities? There was only one way to find out and that was by asking questions.

Before I began with my interrogation, she reached into her purse and pulled out an envelope of photos. That was also ironic because I had prepared a photo album for her that chronicled my life from infancy to just a few months prior to our meeting.

I saw pictures of my nieces and nephews—eleven of them in all—and then she showed me the pictures of my brothers. I was not surprised that I had siblings, but I was amazed at how old these younger brothers looked. Before I asked the age of each one, my eyes rested on a Christmas portrait of one of my brothers and his family.

"Is he the baby?" I inquired, believing him to be the youngest of the three.

"No," she said, as she rubbed my arm affectionately. "You are the baby."

I could not take my eyes off this picture of my older brother as I studied every intricate detail of his face. I looked at his hands, his eyes, his hair and his facial expression as he posed for the photographer. I was entranced, not because I felt like I was staring at my twin, but because I knew I needed to have a normal expression on my face by the time I looked at her again.

He is not the baby, I am! I am the baby and the only girl! The baby! Those were the thoughts that ran through my mind the entire time I looked at the photo. I prayed, *God, please let my face look normal when I glance up at my birth mom, who just told me I was the baby.* As soon as I felt my facial expression would not communicate to her what was happening in my mind, I looked up again.

In all of the years that I imagined meeting my birth mom, I always believed I would have other siblings. It never occurred to me that those siblings would be older. Of all the thoughts that had run rampant through my mind, that was not one of them.

I am the baby?

I am the baby!

As soon as I felt my facial expression would not communicate to her what was happening in my mind, I looked up again.

One week after bringing an unknown situation to the All-Knowing God, I was sitting face-to-face with my birth mother, looking at pictures of my three older brothers and their families.

Not only had He answered my prayer, but He blessed me with more than I could have ever imagined.

The night I offered the contents of my heart to my heavenly Father, He immediately dispatched angels to minister to all parties involved. When I said, "Amen," I was overshadowed with such a peace and presence of God that I did not even worry about the prayer request again.

As I look back on the things that have occurred as a result of the answered prayer, it is impossible for me to have any doubt when I pray.

I had wrestled with questions about my birth family for years, but as soon as I cast those cares upon Jesus, He orchestrated a reunion that still blows my mind ten years later.

The feeling of not being good enough and blaming myself for an event that occurred while I was an infant did not vanish instantaneously, but God always reminded me of the promises found in His word. Before I was conceived He knew me, loved me, and had a great plan for my life.

Those promises are not mine alone. They belong to all who call on the name of Jesus (Romans 10:13; Jeremiah 29:11; Jeremiah 1:5). In spite of the conditions or circumstances of your birth, God is able to make all things beautiful in His time (Ecclesiastes 3:11).

I am a living testimony.

Iris Peterson Bryant is a native of Clinton, North Carolina and has worked as an educator in North Carolina Public Schools for the last twenty-one years. She is involved in the music ministry of Love and Faith Christian Fellowship in Greensboro, NC. She and her husband David are the parents of four children.

Connect with her on her blog: irispbryant.com
Follow her on social media: @irispbryant